OVERTHINKING

How to Stop Destructive Thoughts, Overcome Anxiety,
Declutter Your Mind, and Start Thinking Positively.
A Beginner's Guide That Will Change
How You Think Forever

Richard Campbell with Emma Parker

Table of Contents

INTRODUCTION

Do you find yourself often feeling stressed or panicky? Does it seem like there is never enough time in the day to get things done? Do you spend a lot of time thinking about what disasters could happen? Do you beat yourself up about past mistakes and faux pas? Do you worry to the point where it's excessive about the state of your relationships and how they feel about you on a day to day basis? Is it impossible for you to relax no matter how hard you try?

If you answered yes to most of these things, you are suffering from the habit of overthinking. It causes you to take everything personally. It is what makes you start to worry about your partner being angry with you when they do not text back. It is what makes you cringe at the embarrassing thing you did years ago that everyone else has forgotten about now. It is what gives you that sensation of your heart pounding quickly and your thoughts racing around in a discombobulated mess. Overthinking is very common among people with anxiety. This is because anxiety causes a person to sense danger when there is none.

If you are an overthinker, you are neither alone, nor are you doomed to it forever. This book will teach you what you are going through and how to stop it. To do this, you will need to change your thoughts. Don't worry, this is perfectly doable, and I will show you how.

Chapter 1:

What is Overthinking?

Overthinking causes you to question everything you do. "Did I really lock my door? Did I really turn off the stove? They didn't text me back, what if that means they're angry at me? Does my partner want to break up with me? Are we even meant to be together? Do I even want to be with them? Should I break up with them?"

You see how quickly that spiraled downward. This is what happens when your thoughts become cluttered with anxiety. You begin doubting yourself and the people around you, and before you know it, you are caught in a cycle of thinking in ways that are not good for you. Doubt is a natural part of life. This is because nothing in life is completely certain. We can be assured of the present, and that is what we have to hold on to, no matter how much we want to be able to prevent future misfortunes.

Overthinking begins at a very early age. A child checks their bag and folders for their homework over and over again to make sure they really did complete it and put it where it is supposed to be. They feel a moment of relief when they see their homework in their folder, but shortly after they have zipped up their backpack and are on their way to school, the fear and doubt set in again. They start to wonder if they really did see their homework in that folder. They wonder if they somehow didn't manage to pack it with them even though they checked multiple times. Then they think, "What if it fell out of my folder?" They cannot find any relief from the fear of not having their homework with them until they have turned it in, and then the cycle repeats itself when they get their next assignment.

One way to combat the doubt that you have completed everything you need to for the day is to invest in a planner where you can write down all of your daily tasks. Sometimes it is easier to trust something that is written down on paper than in your mind, which will bombard you with the idea that you missed something. As you mark off the things you have done, you have created evidence that can combat your brain's messages that you must have forgotten something because something feels off.

Just because you feel like something is not right, does not mean this is true. Many times when something bad happens to a person, they say, "I knew that was going to happen. I had a feeling it would." This is impossible. No one can know what the future is going to hold. When you look back at events after they have happened, you can connect the dots, and this can create the illusion of a sixth sense, but unfortunate events are random. You are not chosen for them. If you obsess about forgetting something, you're actually more likely to do so. Think about it this way. When your thoughts are wrapped up in something else, it is easier to miss something.

Overthinking causes you to analyze everything other people do to an agonizing degree. It also causes you to be held hostage by what they are going to say and do next. Let's go back to the person, not replying to your message. As a result of overthinking and coming up with catastrophic reasons as to why this is happening, you will be stuck with anxious feelings and uncertainty until they reply. What if it takes them a day to reply? That means you'll be on edge for a full 24 hours, and this is not factoring in the other things you might be worried about.

How do you tell when you are overthinking? The most noticeable symptom is that you are in a constant state of feeling stressed out.

First, let's delve into what stress really is to gain a better understanding of what it means to have too much of it. Stress in itself is not a bad thing. In fact, in smaller amounts, it can be a good thing because it serves as a stimulator. The true purpose of anxiety is not to be something that is harmful to you, but something that helps you jump into action when you need to. Anxiety has kept the human race alive because it is a means of sensing and responding to threats. An overabundance of anxiety leads to overthinking because it leads you to question everything, even your own self.

Overthinking has been essentially broken down into two different types. One of them is shaming yourself about things that have happened in the past. That includes feeling embarrassed about the things you've done in the past and feeling ashamed for the mistakes you have made.

The other is worrying about the things that could happen in the future. You worry about what may happen with the weather. You worry about what other people will do. You fear for problems to come about in your interpersonal relationships. There is no evidence that these things are even going to happen.

Overthinking does no favors for you. Think about how much time and energy it takes away from you. It consumes so many of your resources and doesn't give you anything in return.

Reading this book is a proactive thing you have done. It means you are taking an active role in your recovery. I am not going to sugarcoat this. Breaking the habit of overthinking will not happen overnight, nor will it be any small feat. You will need to commit fully to this. When a person stops abusing a substance all in once, it is known as "quitting cold turkey," and it is known as something that is nearly impossible to do. You cannot quit cold turkey when it comes to overthinking. It just won't happen. At this point, it is an involuntary action. Your tendency to personalize the things other people do has become second nature. Visions of a catastrophic future and unpleasant memories from the past bombard you, and you don't know how to stop them.

The harsh truth is that we cannot stop unpleasant thoughts from entering our minds. We have anywhere from 50,000 to 80,000 thoughts every day. You cannot monitor all of them. There will always be times where you have thoughts that are unwanted. The trick is to change the way you respond to them. Trying to make these thoughts go away by pushing on them will not work. When you try to forbid yourself from thinking about something, it is the only thing you will want to think about. Instead, you will need to learn to accept them as they come. You can acknowledge their presence without giving them your full attention.

Let's say you have the recurring thought that your house will be struck by a tornado. This is a very distressing thought, and as you immerse yourself into it and conjure up the images of it happening. It can start to feel very real as you imagine your house being consumed by the storm. If you dwell in this thought, you will begin to feel despair. That is when you need to pull yourself back to reality. Look at your surroundings. Everything is firmly on the ground. The sky is clear, and even if it is not, it is only raining. There is nothing that indicates a tornado. This means the fear responses going on in your body are inaccurate. You cannot always trust the messages your body and your brain send to you for they are not always accurate. You need to examine their messages and see if there is any evidence that could support their validity. If there is none, the thought can be discarded.

In the society we live in today, we are prone to information overload. This is one of the things that contributes to overthinking. In earlier times, we were only exposed to what was happening in our lives and the towns we lived in. Now, with the internet giving us access to information all the way across the world, it also burdens us with the knowledge of everything that happens in the world. Every time something bad happens, we hear about it. If there is a huge car collision that caused a lot of damage, we hear about it. If a scandal comes out about a beloved and trusted public figure doing criminal or immoral activities, it becomes worldwide news. We hear about it every time someone goes missing, or if someone snaps and does something violent, that affects a large group of people. When things like these happen, the news goes covers it over and over again. Sometimes entire days or even weeks are dedicated to the scandal if it's big enough. The stories of terrorists and serial killers are remembered and told throughout the ages, long after they have died, the tales of their grisly deeds painted in vivid detail on the television screen as they are portrayed by well-known actors.

All of this talk about bad things happening all over the world can create the idea within us that the world is a dangerous place, which builds up a fear of it. This is one of the ways overthinking is created and perpetuated. It's a good thing to keep up with current events, but you do not need to tune into every single thing that is said and every detail that comes up about the crime or scandal. There comes a point where any new information about the case will only be something that causes you additional pain and stress.

That is where we learn when to distance ourselves from the news. It leads people into discussions that can become inflammatory, and often you have to wait a little while before you get the full story. You've probably heard the twisting and turning of events and multiple versions of a big story. For example, when there is large crime discovered, there will be stories that say relatives of the person had no idea it was going on, and then there will be stories that they were in on it. Some people will write out their theories that government officials and even celebrities were in on it. They will point out flimsy evidence behind their claims, which are designed to fill your head with doubts.

When you hear about too many crimes at once, it will become frightening to even step outside of your house. People who suffer from overthinking do this, especially because they are more affected by disturbing stories than everyone else. For other people, they will have a little while where they are bothered by it, but eventually, their focus on it tapers out.

When you are an overthinker, you can become consumed by it. It can affect your ability to eat and sleep. Some people even report that the only way they can stop being plagued by one disturbing thought is to replace it by discovering something even worse.

People who overthink blame themselves for everything that goes on around them. Often it starts from childhood. Think of the child whose parents are getting a divorce, and they feel like this wouldn't be happening had they been a better child. They might think if their own behavior improves, their parents' marriage will be saved. They do not realize their parents' relationship has nothing to do with them. This is exacerbated when the parents drag their child into the arguments. This can take the form of fighting in front of them and badmouthing the other parent to their child. In particularly sick situations, the parents even use their child to relay unkind messages to one another. For some couples, it still isn't over after they get a divorce. They try to pump their child for information about the other parent and engage in a long, drawn-out custody battle where both parties fight dirty. A child's mind is easily warped by this. They will think they played a role in the collapse of their parents' marriage.

Another problem people who overthink struggle with is one they find hard to talk about. It is something that happens to everyone, but for people who cannot let go of thoughts, it can be debilitating. Once in a while, a thought will pop into your mind that is unusual and not reflective of the person's true nature.

If you had thought of yourself dressing up as a unicorn out in public, you would probably just laugh it as an odd thought. You probably wouldn't question why you had that thought and wonder if there was a part of you that secretly wanted to go outside dressed as a unicorn. This is because this thought is not a disturbing one.

Sometimes overthinking leads to people having doubts about themselves. One of the most common ways this kind of thinking infiltrates a person's mind is to attack their romantic relationship, making them doubt it. Everyone has doubts sometimes when the relationship isn't going well, or even as just a passing thought because choosing one person to be with for the rest of your life is a big decision, and you want to be sure you made the right one. However, overthinking comes in the form of a sudden, jarring thought such as "Is there any chance they're cheating on me or don't love me anymore?" or "What if I don't really love them?" A thought like this could ruin your day and make you wonder if your whole life was a lie.

Overthinking is sustained by the idea that thoughts and feelings are indicative of reality. This is sometimes referred to as emotional reasoning. This is a destructive way of thinking because it encourages you to take your thoughts at face value rather than questioning them, which you should do. You need to question your thoughts, feelings, and even your impulses to see if they are real because they are sometimes another product of information overload.

Let's say that question does come into your mind- "Do I really love my spouse?" The thought itself would be jarring, and you would be thinking to yourself, "why did I have that thought? What does it say about me that I did? There must be a problem in my relationship if my mind would even go there?" This could lead to questioning where you and your partner stand when, in reality, nothing has changed. There is nothing wrong with your relationship except that you had a random, meaningless thought. You might have watched a movie about a toxic marriage. Maybe a couple you know is having problems or going through a divorce and giving public updates about it. Either of these things would cause you to have relationship troubles on the brain. Seeing other people go through these kinds of problems will naturally make you look at your own relationship with a more critical eye. It might also simply make the thought pass through your mind at some point during the day, just as watching a scary movie has the potential to make you have strange or disturbing passing thoughts.

It might seem like a stretch that movies and TV would influence your thoughts, but the human brain is influenced by everything we see and hear to some extent. Think about it this way. Movies have the power to make people laugh or cry. Songs have the power to make you want to reconnect with people you parted ways with. People develop lifelong feelings for fictional characters, whether they are good, bad, or a mixture of the two. Art has an impact on us.

I'm not going to reassure you that nothing bad will ever happen because I can't. Sometimes bad things happen, and there is no explanation for them, nor is there any preventing them. What I can promise you, however, is that these events are the exception, not the rule. Don't limit your life based on fear. The hard truth is that you could never leave your house trying to stay safe, and when someone breaks in, but the chances of this really happening are slim to none. You need to make the decision about what force is going to be in control when you act, your fear or your desires. This isn't to say not to go into things with open eyes, but if you have anxiety, you have that part down. We must also learn to go into things with open eyes. The saying "you can't be too careful" isn't entirely accurate. You can be so careful that you miss out on living your life to the fullest. In fact, it is a part of growing up. A child acts based on what is safe and won't get them into trouble. An adult act based on what they want to do.

Overthinking tries to take the fun out of everything for you. You fear of going to the beach out of the fear of sharks or other underwater creatures. For many people with anxiety, there is a big trepidation about driving because they fear making a mistake and getting into an accident. They might avoid going to social events because their mind goes to the idea that someone with ill intentions can be there. They miss out on opportunities for social life expansion and romance because they avoid pursuing them out of the fear of rejection.

If you are interested in someone, ask them out. The worst thing they can tell you is no. There is also the chance they will say yes. Either way, you will have your answer. You will have a date with someone you like, or you will not waste any more time, and that leaves you free to explore things with other people who are interested in you.

Overthinking mimics OCD in the sense that people who struggle with it are plagued with doubts about everything-their relationships, their careers, their safety, the safety of their loved ones, even their own sanity. Overthinking is an abnormal thought process, but it is not a sign of insanity. As the thoughts become scarier, you might feel like you are going to lose your mind, which only heightens the anxiety. Thoughts do not make you crazy. They do not make you anything because they are not a reflection of your true character.

Let's say you want to sing in front of people, but are convinced that you will not be able to work up the courage to do it. You might deem yourself as not being confident enough because you have thoughts in your head that make you nervous about doing something that involves getting in front of a group of people. These thoughts do not define you as a person. You might think people who sing on stage are able to do so because they are not nervous, but this almost never true. No matter how many times a performer does their act, they will still be nervous before they get on stage. It is a natural feeling. In fact, some of your favorite singers might feel very anxious before getting onstage. Some even become physically ill out of worry. They might have the thought cross their mind a thousand times before and even as they walk in front of their audience: "I can't do this, this is too much." However, they are able to go out there and put on a show because their thoughts are not a true reflection of who they are. The thought "I can't do this" goes through their mind as a response to the fear in their minds. That is all it is.

Figuring out where you are going, what you want to do, and the meaning you want to attach to your life will make it seem simpler. Do not put too much pressure on it or think this has to be a one-time and permanent event. Finding your life's purpose isn't a one-time adventure. It can change over time. We don't stay the same person our whole lives. We all go through times where something that interested us at one point is no longer enjoyable. This is a normal thing. We also find new hobbies and interests. It is never too late to discover another part of yourself.

You do not need to let anxiety control anything you do, and this book is intended to show you just what it is that you are going through and how to overcome it.

Chapter 2:
Anxiety and Its Causes

In order to treat your anxiety, you need to know where it is coming from. Many people describe it as feeling random. It might seem this way because the onset can seem to be out of nowhere. Overthinking causes and contributes to anxiety. They have a relationship to where they both feed off of one another. If you have anxiety, you have a predisposition to overthinking, meanwhile overthinking will increase your levels of anxiety.

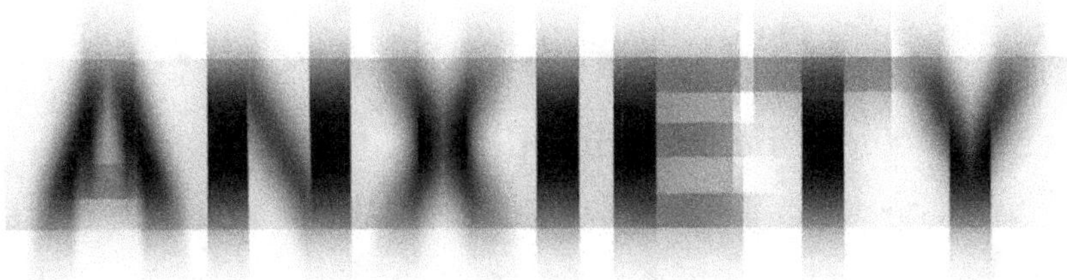

There is a reason people who suffer from anxiety disorder are especially prone to overthinking. This is because their mind has become trained to think in worst-case scenarios. For example, they might be driving, and if they feel the bumps that sometimes happen when you're out on the road, and their mind goes to the idea that they hit something. Let me reassure you of something. You would not think you might have hit something or someone. The impact would be like no other. Not everything can be prevented because things happen sometimes, but as long as you are looking at the road ahead of you and do not have any chemicals in your system that could impede your cognitive function, it is unlikely that you are going to get into any serious accident.

Most of the time, it is not random when a person develops anxiety. Sometimes it comes as a delayed reaction of sorts. You might not feel the effects of it while you're going through a stressful situation because your mind is primarily focused on getting through the situation. After the fact, you go through the psychological effects of your situation because you have time to think about it. This is a common thing that happens to people during stressful situations. We stuff our feelings about it because we want to focus on thinking pragmatically and getting ourselves into a better place.

There have been findings that there are certain chemicals in our brain that can cause mood and emotional disorders when off-kilter. However, there also tends to be an environmental component. There are things that can happen to a person that makes them more likely to have difficulty handling stress. That lies where anxiety becomes a disorder. At a certain level, it is natural. When it passes that point and becomes a hindrance in a person's life, it has become a disorder.

Here's essentially how it works. You have an assignment that is due in two weeks. A healthy level of anxiety will make you think, "okay, I need to do this much work in this amount of time. If I want to make the deadline and put out good work, I can't wait around until the last minute. I need to do this much work every day to reach my goals." When it gets to be about the middle of the day, and you haven't done it yet, you start to feel a little uneasy and remind yourself that you need to get going. It's like a person inside you giving you a nudge to get started on your responsibilities because they want to see you succeed. When an anxiety disorder takes over, you will be overcome with fear when you see the requirements and the deadline. You might think, "there's no way I can handle all of this. How will I come up with that much material in such a short amount of time?" Every time you begin to work on it, the blank page intimidates you, and you decide you'd rather spend your time doing something that does not cause you so much stress. Just the thought of working on it makes your heart rate go up. You tell yourself, "I can't handle this today, I'm going to work on it tomorrow when I'm stronger." Then tomorrow comes, and you use the same excuse to put it off.

Any number of things can cause an anxiety disorder. Everyone has times in their lives when their anxiety is at a heightened level. Major life events, such as illness in the family or the loss of a relationship, come with stress naturally. Even good things like getting a new job can cause anxiety.

One of the biggest reasons endings and new beginnings cause anxiety is because then the question becomes, "What comes next?" People have a natural fear of the unknown. Thinking about the new job, you might be confused because you don't know why you aren't jumping for joy. This might be your first job out of school, or it might be a major upgrade from your last one. The working conditions are better, the pay is higher, and your benefits are greater. However, you don't know exactly how this job is going to be. You might have read what will be expected of you in your new role, but that isn't the same as actually being in the job and going through the motions. You haven't met your coworkers yet, and you have only met your boss very briefly. You might have had to move for this job, so that means you're in a whole new environment. You're in a new neighborhood with people you've never met before, and you will have to find where everything is. You're hoping you don't get lost on your first day at work. Is it now becoming more understandable why you'd be nervous about starting a new job?

Sometimes anxiety disorders are born from trauma. When you think of trauma, you probably think of horrible assaults and natural disasters. While these would definitely be a source of anxiety, don't write off your experiences as not being enough to be trauma. If you had a parent who had a short temper and yelled often, and these temper tantrums didn't take much to provoke, it's easy to see where that would leave you with anxiety. You would be unsure of your social interactions. You would interpret everything people do that seems off as a sign that they are about to become angry because you had been exposed to so much anger.

Thinking about the past can bring on anxiety. It can influence your future. Say you did poorly on your most recent exam. If you spend all of your time beating yourself up about it, you will actually be lowering your motivation to do better next time rather than increasing it. Every time you try to study for the next exam, your mind will go back to the last grade, which will distract you from learning new information. Your morale will be low, and that will decrease your self-confidence. People who do not feel good about themselves will not put in their maximum efforts in what they do because they do not feel that they will do well anyways.

There is no undoing the past. Whether your test score was poor because you didn't study as much as you should have, or you studied the wrong material or didn't get enough sleep, or anything else that could've contributed to the failing grade, you can't go back in time and study properly for your previous exam. That is done. Acknowledging what you did wrong in the past should be an aid in doing better in the future, not an instrument to punish yourself.

The fact that you cannot change the past might be discouraging, but try thinking about it in a different way. If we could go back in time and change what we have done, which we can't, we would never be able to start a new beginning because we would be so consumed with fixing what has already happened. Then, what would be the point of improving as a person? You wouldn't have to because you could just turn back time and act differently, which might change the future in ways you wouldn't expect or want.

The permanent state of the past lifts a burden for everyone it places on us. The only thing we need to worry about is the present and how it will affect the future. Let's say you failed that exam because you spent a little too much time playing video games and too little time studying for it. You know what went wrong. Use the errors of the past in that way only. Use them for finding out how you got the undesired outcome so you can prevent getting a similar one later on. This doesn't mean you have a serious problem with gaming or that you need to give it up altogether. It means you need to find a way to incorporate it into your life so that it doesn't impede other aspects of it. Schedule the time you are going to fit into your day that is reserved for gaming and do not let it go past that. Make sure you have done everything you need to do before you start to do the things you want to.

Make a checklist for yourself about what tasks you need to complete before the end of the day. When you find out what material will be on your next exam, begin setting aside a few hours per day to study. If you have homework, get it done before you log into your game accounts. It can be tempting to start indulging in your hobbies when you get home, but there are a few problems with this. If you do wind up getting to your homework or whatever other things you need to do, you will probably wind up putting it off until it's nearly midnight. Once you get it done, it will probably be early in the morning, and then it will take you a little while after that to get to sleep. You will wake up the next morning feeling tired and groggy, and the work you did last night will have been done with a tired mind. Another possibility is that it will be nearly midnight and you'll decide you're too tired to do it tonight, and therefore put it off until tomorrow morning. This causes you to spend the next morning completing your assignment in a blur, and that is if you have enough time to do so and don't have to hand in a paper that has objectives that go uncompleted.

You will actually have more time to indulge in your hobbies and have more fun doing them if you do what you need to do first. If you have the fact that you have some homework you need to do while you are playing your games, the whole experience will be a stressful one because the thought is always hanging over your head- "When am I going to put away the game and get to my assignments? I'll do it right after this match. No, I'm just going to do one more, and then I'll get to it. Okay, I've got 4 hours to it, I've got plenty of time. I still have three hours. I'll play for just a little bit longer. Oh no! I only have half an hour left! Where did the time go? I have to start now! Please let me finish on time."

The very stress of the situation will cause you to stay in your gaming and not tackle your homework. You think, "it's too stressful to think about doing that assignment, and this is relaxing me, so I'm going to keep doing it." However, you're not really relaxed. You can't be because you have a thought looming over you and nagging you in the back of your mind. The stress builds underneath because you know that no amount of doing nothing is going to make that assignment go away. In fact, the more time that passes, the more real it gets because you know you can only put it off for so long.

Keeping a schedule and sticking with it will take a very heavy weight off of your mind. It will also give you a sense of accomplishment. As you check things off your to-do list because you have completed them will make you feel more confident. When the list has been completed, you will feel good about yourself when you go to bed because you will know you have done everything you need to do.

Young adults often feel a great deal of anxiety due to social expectations. The way society is now; you are viewed as a child who needs to ask permission to do anything until you turn 18. At this point, you are seen as an adult in the eyes of the law, and now you are being expected to find out what you are going to do with your life. You've needed to go to your teacher for a bathroom pass, and now you're being bombarded with questions about what you are going to do in the way of a career. You go off to college, where you find out that you need to occupy yourself, and you also are solely responsible for making sure you have all your assignments done on time and know everything you will need to do in the near future. That has not been the case in the past. This is overwhelming. However, at least during your college years, there is a resemblance to your old life. Afterward is when many people find themselves feeling lost.

There is a growing problem following college graduation where people go through a period of not knowing what to do. They are struggling to find a job that is related to the field they got their degree in, or any job at all. This inspires depression, as well as anxiety. In fact, that is why it has earned the name "the post-graduation depression." Graduates feel depressed because they have nothing to do and as a result of the guilt they feel for not having "launched" yet. It is also a time of great fear. You are wondering if you are ever going to be able to start your life. You may be feeling pressure from your parents to get your career started because they are looking at your situation using their own memory of when they were your age, not realizing the economy and society have changed since then, and it is much more difficult for a person to get started with their life now.

It is also easy to let the anxiety about the future cause you to avoid thinking about it. Many people fall into the rut where they let days go by without job searching because it feels too stressful. In a way, it is a retreat into oneself. There are some ways to keep yourself from slipping into this and to get out of it if that's where you're at.

First, go to sleep at a reasonable time and get up early in the morning. When you are nervous about your future, you can find yourself in a habit where you fall asleep at a very late hour and then sleep until sometime in the afternoon. This is an avoidance tactic because then you can say, "Well, it's too late to go job hunting now, the day is almost over." You can' avoid your life. It will happen with or without you in the driver's seat. Set a certain number of job applications per day. Eventually, someone will say yes.

Also, think about exploring alternative career paths. For example, if you excel in writing, or just have an interest in it, you might want to consider freelance writing. You might choose to supplement your income with it, and for some people, it is their full-time career. It might seem impossible to start, but once you get that first client, you've gotten a foot in. Then you will find your second client. Most companies need a writer. You can be a blogger, a technical writer, a fictional writer, anything you can possibly think of; there is a niche for it in the writing business.

While you are searching for your career, do not beat yourself up about where you are compared to everyone else. You are where you are, and that is fine. Before you get started, use the time you have in between for self-discovery. Once you get into the workforce, it will be a consistent thing, so use this time in between for self-betterment. Figure out who you are, and not just in terms of finding your career. In fact, when you have done some self-reflection, it might be easier to find what you want to do with your life. Feel free to try a few career paths before you settle on one. Think long and hard about whether this is something you could see yourself doing long-term. Do not beat yourself up about what you haven't done. That won't get you anywhere. Celebrate what you have done, and know that you are going to do more in the future.

Holding wasted time against you is pointless and will only lead to wasting more time. It is a road to nowhere. Making yourself suffer over a mistake does not undo it. Treat yourself the way you would a close friend who had made a mistake. You would not remind them over and over of the things they did wrong, and if someone tried to do that, you would probably stand up for them and tell that person they couldn't talk to your friend that way. Be a friend to yourself. Stand up for yourself and tell that voice in your mind it doesn't get to insult you, and you take it lying down. Let it know you will make up your own mind about yourself and that your self-esteem will have nothing to do with any unkind remarks it makes.

The most important thing to remember is that once you have improved your behavior, you need to congratulate yourself on that instead of focusing on the errors of the past. Not only will you not undo those mistakes, but you will prevent yourself from achieving future successes. Absolve yourself of the past so your focus can be on the future.

CHAPTER 3:

OUTSIDE FACTORS- THINGS WE CAN'T CONTROL

Overthinking sustains itself on worrying about things that are beyond a person's control. You worry about your friend who has been doing poorly in school because they aren't doing their assignments and are at the risk of failing. You're afraid of what the weather is going to do tomorrow and if it is going to force you to cancel your plans. You worry about your friend and whether or not they are ever going to get out of that relationship where they are consistently cheated on. The list goes on. The problem is that you don't have any control over any of these things. The weather is going to do whatever it wants to do, just like your friends will do.

You cannot control what other people are going to do. You can tell them how you feel about what they are doing, but that is the only influence you have over their decisions. In fact, the more you interfere, the more it will hurt your spirit because you will feel like you are not being heard, and the constant disagreement will have a negative impact on your friendship with them.

Imagine you have a friend who is in a relationship with someone you think is toxic for them. Your first instinct might be to yell at your friend until you are blue in the face to break it off with that person and give them all of your reasons for thinking they should. You might think it would be the best thing for them, and it might be true, but it's not your call. Trying to forbid someone to see someone else will only create what is sometimes called "the Romeo and Juliet effect." Your distaste for their relationship will only make that person more appealing to your friend. In addition, you will alienate them by doing this. They will become angry at you for trying to make decisions about their life, which ultimately is what you are doing. Your stress is heightened because not only are you worried about their relationship but now you fear for your own relationship with them because they are upset with you.

People with anxiety have a hard time letting go of control. There might have been a time in your life where you felt like you had very little control over your life, and now that is manifesting in the need to micromanage everything around you today. This becomes frustrating because then you realize you can't impact or prevent the things you are trying to.

One of the worst things you can do for your mental well-being is to create potential disasters in your mind and treat them as if they are things that are bound to happen at any given moment.

These catastrophic scenarios vary depending on the person. The one consistent theme is that they would be disastrous events from this person's point of view. It might be a literal natural disaster such as a tornado or a hurricane. For people with social anxiety, they live with a constant fear of embarrassing themselves in a social situation, which could cause them to avoid any interactions with other people that they can. A common fear for people with anxiety centers around their romantic relationships, which means they feel a constant worry that their partner has lost interest in them and is having thoughts about breaking it off with them.

It's normal to sometimes have fears creep into your mind. It happens to everyone. The presence of insecurity doesn't inherently mean you are overthinking. It is when it becomes a hindrance to your daily life that it becomes a problem.

Overthinking is when a thought becomes an obsession. This is what makes it akin to obsessive-compulsive disorder, or OCD. In fact, it mimics the symptoms of OCD. It is a commonly misunderstood disorder. Many times when people hear about OCD, they imagine someone who obsessively cleans their house and not is satisfied until there isn't a speck of dirt to be found anywhere in it. They imagine a person arranging everything on their desk to where they all line up perfectly. While the obsessions can sometimes take on the form of being fixated on cleanliness, it sometimes has nothing to do with this theme, and if the obsession does happen to be about being tidy, it will go much deeper than just being a neat-freak. The person feels like there will be dire consequences for failing to keep the place in order, such as bad things happening to the people they care about. They feel like they are responsible for everything that happens around them. When something bad happens to someone else, they blame themselves for it. They think there's something they could have done to prevent it. It also means they assign powers to themselves that they do not really have.

People who suffer from the habit of overthinking are often unsure of themselves and wonder if they had a role in a tragedy even when they were nowhere near the event. You need to get out of the habit of holding yourself accountable for the things that happen around you. There are certain things that will happen, no matter what you do or don't do. Many times people who overthink fall into a mental trap of thinking their worrying about something has the power to prevent it. Let's say you do not worry about your friend's health for a day, and they get a cold. It might be tempting to blame yourself and think because you took a break from worrying about them getting sick, you are responsible for what happened to them. There are a few reasons this is not true. Your thought processes are not related to what happens to another person in terms of their physical health. Other than avoiding them while you are under the weather, there is nothing you personally can do to keep another person from getting sick. They probably got it from someone coughing at the store, or because they touched something that had also been touched by someone who was sick. It also might have been something as simple as the fact that it is allergy season, and sickness is spreading around. Any number of things could have been the cause of this that had nothing to do with you.

When we overthink, we make connections between events that are not there.

If someone is making a bad decision about their life, it is not because you didn't try hard enough to talk them out of it. For example, you have a friend who is not doing well in school because they are not applying themselves. Instead of studying for their tests and doing their homework, they are going to parties and hanging out with people who do not have their best interests at heart. When you try to talk to them or spend time with them, they avoid you and try to figure out a way to get out of the conversation. Soon it comes out that they are failing their classes and on academic probation. Before you start to think this is because there was something you did or did not do, you need to think about this. Everyone is responsible for their own lives. This means they are the only ones who have control over their actions and choices. You can try to talk someone out of making a bad decision, but in the end, if their mind is made up, they will do what they want to do.

There are certain people whose opinions you need to care about. You should be concerned with what kind of impression you make on a potential employer. You should worry about the state of your relationship with the people who care about you and support you in your endeavors. You should not worry about what random people think about you. If you are out at a restaurant, do not let your evening be ruined by someone at the table across the room, which you've never met before and will probably never see again after tonight. You might think they are looking at you because they have some sort of problem with you, but there might be another explanation. For one, they might not actually be looking at you, but something else that is in your general direction. They might also be looking at you because you look like someone they know. It might even be something positive. They might like your outfit and want to know where you got it. It is very unlikely that someone you don't know doesn't like you on sight.

Also, think about this. Let's say the worst-case scenario is true, and they are staring at you with distaste for some unknown reason. How much is this going to really affect you? After tonight their impact on your life is most likely over. If you do not concentrate on them, and instead just enjoy your meal and the company you are with while eating it, this person cannot have any effect on you.

In a perfect world, everyone would get along with everyone, and we would never come across someone who didn't like us. That's not the way the real world works, though. Sometimes we will meet people, and for some reason, they will have a distaste for us. You might never know why they don't like you, and you don't need to know their reasons, because they are just one person. While you can perfect your social skills, practice your empathy and try to be friendly, for some people, this just won't be enough. If you try to make everyone like you, you will end up being a people-pleaser. Over time you will begin to lose the sense of your authentic self. Other people have only the power over you that you give them.

It would be great if we could predict when bad things were about to happen and what they would be, but this isn't something anyone can do. You also don't want to be constantly preparing for them either because this can quickly develop into paranoia.

Paranoia is probably a universal problem for people who overthink. This state of mind is characterized by intense anxiety. You start assuming the worst in every situation. One of the most defining traits of paranoia is having feelings of persecution. This means you feel like people are out to get you. Paranoia causes you to personalize everything other people do. You are filled with a dread that your friends don't really like you. Sometimes these feelings are baseless, or they come from something that is benign.

You cannot let yourself sink into paranoia. It is a miserable state to be in. It prevents you from being happy. When you start to have a good day, it can be ruined by one thing another person says or any little inconvenience. For example, sometimes it gets to the point where people think because they spilled coffee on themselves this morning or they slept past their alarm, this is an omen or a message sent from the universe that it is going to be a bad day.

The universe doesn't send messages to anyone personally. Things just happen sometimes, and we can't always control it. Thinking the world or a higher power in it has something against you and wants to hurt you specifically is completely unproductive. It is easy to think bad things happen only to you and not to other people. This is because you know about every experience you go through, but you do not see the things that happen to other people. When you see your coworkers show up to work every day, they might have had car troubles or been in a traffic jam on the way there, causing them to worry about whether they were going to be able to get to work on time. You might look at your friend's pictures of their spouse, children, and pets on their social media and feel envious of them, thinking they must have everything you don't and be oblivious to the misfortunes you have. However, you only see a portion of the story. You don't see the disagreements they have. You don't see them when they are not having a good time. Every family has its crises. Every marriage or relationship has its own unique problems. You don't see what other people struggle with because we live in a society that values appearances. This means we portray our lives in the best light possible. Before we take a picture, we make sure we look our best and clean up the space that will be shown in the photo. When we have a good evening, we post about that, and if some words come out wrong over the course of the evening, we do not mention that part. In fact, other people might look at your life with envy and think you do not have any problems. They might wish their relationship looked more like yours. No one has a perfect life, and no one has everything figured out.

Bad things happen to everyone pretty consistently, but the reverse is also true. Good things happen to you every day. To build up your optimism, think about the good things that happened to you today. Compile a list of them. It doesn't have to be long. Also, broaden your definition of what counts as something good that happened to you. You might not have won the lottery or find the love of your life, but maybe someone complimented your outfit. Maybe you dropped a coin, and someone picked it up for you. Maybe lunch was especially good today, or you got a good seat on the bus. It could be something as simple as you having seen a beautiful flower.

As an overthinker, you probably do not prioritize yourself as much as you should. You worry about how other people are doing, but have not stopped to think about taking care of yourself. In the end, people are where they want to be. Your friend might have a long list of complaints about their relationship, but in the end, if they refuse to leave them, that is their decision. Sometimes people just have to learn things the hard way. If they decide to change their course of action, it won't be because of anything someone else said to them.

If you think someone is making a poor decision, here is what you can do. Tell them what you feel about it and what you would do if you were them. Say it in a neutral voice, and then let it go. After you have given someone your advice about what they should do, you have done everything you can for them. Letting it go is the only thing you can do that will keep you sane.

Change your priority list. Instead of trying to advise people who don't want to be advised, think about what you want to do for yourself today. Think about if you are getting enough sleep or eating right. Your well-being has to come first.

You will become a much happier person when you worry about your own business first. Then you will not be chasing someone else around talking until you are blue in the face only for them not to listen. You will no longer be losing sleep, helping people who wouldn't do the same for you. When you put yourself first and let other people do what they will, you will not have a front-row seat to everything bad that happens.

Sometimes the best thing we can do for another person is to let them make their mistakes. They might come back to you later after having learned their lesson, and you can rekindle your friendship. They might never get to this point, and you have to distance yourself from them. Either way, your number one priority needs to be your own well-being. You do not know what is going on in other people's minds, and there is no way to figure it out. That is why it is so important to be in touch with what you are feeling and what you want, and let other things happen as they do. You might have to change your plans according to what happens in the outside world, but then you will have the opportunity to adjust to these changes in a way that is good for you.

Overthinkers take other people's decisions, especially rejection, especially hard. They personalize it. Say you get laid off from your job because the company was required to make some hard decisions. It is very likely that you were not laid off because your boss has a personal grudge against you. It probably isn't anything at all against you. It is never an easy conversation to tell someone they have lost their job, and they certainly didn't enjoy giving you this information.

While job hunting, overthinkers need to watch out to avoid getting discouraged after their application is denied. You might feel like no one will hire you. Recent college graduates are especially vulnerable to falling into this mentality. You might feel like you are behind your peers in getting your life started and wonder if there is something wrong with you because you haven't found a job yet. Did you know it takes most people at least a year after getting their Bachelor's degree to find work, and for some people, it takes even longer?

That is a lie your mind will tell you if you are struggling or not at the place in life you want to be- "I'm the only one." For a college graduate, they might think, "I'm the only one who hasn't gotten a job yet. Everyone else has a high-paying job in the field of their degree, and I'm living with my parents."

You are only one struggling. In fact, no one really has everything together. We all struggle in our own ways. Everyone is behind in one way or another. Thinking about what other people have and you don't will only cause you pain. Don't think about where you should be or what other people are doing. Only focus on where you are right now and what you can currently influence. The past, the distant future, and the choices other people make are all things that you have no say in.

Chapter 4:
Self-Created Factors-
What We Can Control

The last chapter was not meant to be discouraging. In fact, it is meant to be liberating. When you realize the things you can't have any impact on, you have time to work on the things you can.

Overthinking leads you to believe you are powerless in your own life. You might think you are stuck in unhappy situations. This is not true. There are changes you can make to your life to improve it. It is not always about making monumental changes to what you do. Sometimes changing little habits can brighten your day.

A major culprit in anxiety is procrastination, or avoiding responsibilities. Everyone has struggled with procrastination at one point. Sometimes we're not sure what we're supposed to do, so we put off doing it. Sometimes it's because we simply don't want to do it. However, for some people, it is a habit. Every time they get a project they end up putting it off until the last minute. Then they have to do the entire project in one panicked sitting, praying the whole time they can just create enough content. If they do send it in on time, it is unedited and probably full of errors. They don't even feel relieved because they know they will do poorly on the assignment.

Sometimes we procrastinate because the entire task seems daunting. Imagine you have to write a 3,000-word paper. While you are staring at a blank page, you feel intimidated, and you wonder how you are going to get it all done in time. The harsh truth is that no amount of worrying will get any words on that page. Let's say you have 20 days to do it. If you divide the number of words by the number of days you have, it will come out to 150 words per day. That seems a lot less scary, doesn't it? Treat every project this way. Figure out what you need to get done and how long you have to do it. When you do this, the days will not pass by, and the due date will not sneak up on you. That's how we end up having to do the entire thing at the last minute. We shrug off another day, saying to ourselves, "There's still time to do it." The problem with that mentality is that there will inevitably come a point where there is no more time.

Let's go back to that paper. You write 150 words a day. The average typing speed is 40 words per minute. Along with whatever research you need to do, the actual typing will only take about four minutes of your day, give or take. This will give you plenty of time to proofread and revise what you have written. On the day the paper is due, you will be able to hand in work you have confidence in. When you do turn it in, you will be at ease, and then you can enjoy the rest of your day.

Then imagine you put it all off until the last day. The paper will be something you have to dedicate your entire day to. You will not proofread anything. Your only goal will be meeting the word count. This means your paper will undoubtedly be filled with grammatical errors and poorly structured sentences. Your mind will outrun your fingers, which means you might not even complete the thought on the page before you start the next one, leaving you with incomplete sentences. Not only will it be possibly unreadable, but you will be doing minimal research, meaning you won't know what you're talking about. You will have to resort to being overly wordy and writing nonsense in order to achieve 3,000 words. Your professor will know the second they begin to read it that this was a paper that was written at the last minute, and they will grade it as such.

Which scenario sounds better to you?

Next, let's talk about how other people's decisions actually present an opportunity for you. You can't control what other people do, but you can control your response to it. Sometimes, that means giving them a break. No one can live up to the standards that your mindsets for other people. There is a negative meaning attached to everything they don't do perfectly. If they fail to reply to you, they must be upset with you. If they don't respond with the right amount of enthusiasm to something, you say they must secretly disagree with you. If they get distracted for a moment, they must be bored with everything you say. No one could ever possibly live up to the standard of responding on time every time without fail, never getting distracted, and always emoting exactly to the degree that reassures you.

Remember that we're all humans. We make mistakes. We miss cues and say the wrong thing. We can't always live up to the expectations of others. Have you ever had a time where you ignored someone's message because you were just too tired or stressed to deal with anything at the moment?

When you suffer from anxiety, you tend to jump to the worst possible conclusion. You will need to challenge these thoughts because they serve no purpose for you. Before assuming your friend is angry at you for replying, try to think of other possible explanations. They might have gotten busy. They might have fallen asleep after a long day at school or work. They might be struggling with a problem that is distracting them from their usual activities. They might have simply thought they had sent the text back and forgotten to press the send button. There are many things that could have happened other than them having become upset with you.

Jumping to conclusions is one of the ways overthinking leads to irrational thinking. Think of a time you were at a restaurant, and it was taking a long time for the food to come out. You didn't assume it was something the waiter was doing to spite you, did you? Your mind probably didn't go there because you could see that there were a lot of customers or maybe they were serving a large table today. The waiter had never met you in their life so it was impossible that they would deny you your food out of spite. Apply this thinking to other situations in your life.

When you stop overthinking, you become more understanding of the people around you. When someone is not acting like themselves, you will no longer automatically assume that they are angry with you, which will leave room for you trying to understand what is the true reason for their change in behavior. If a person is continually breaking commitments with you and has been unavailable lately, and this is not their usual behavior, it probably is not about you. You might find out they are going through a breakup or divorce, or that they have a family member who is sick, or that they are not doing well financially. Instead of personalizing their behavior, ask them if there's anything they need to talk about. Let them know you're there for them. You will come out of it as closer friends.

You will spend a lot of time feeling anxious about what others may not ever even do or say if you continue to overthink. You will be putting yourself in a position where you are powerless over your own mood. In a way, you get to blame others for the things you are feeling. "I'm feeling anxious because they're not responding." "I'm upset because they're acting a certain way." If you let outside forces have power over you, you will never be able to be in a sustainable good mood. Also, don't put too much pressure on days and events. If you are with a group of friends at lunch and no one is talking, don't assume that is because no one is having fun. Sometimes there is just comfortable silence. Everyone might be enjoying the food so much that they don't want to do anything but eat it.

Don't underestimate the way your views on the past can influence your future. You can't change the past, but you can change your view on it. If you spend a lot of time thinking about an embarrassing moment from a long time ago, it doesn't change anything. However, you can change the way an unwanted memory such as this affects you. Let's say you tripped over and fell in front of your coworkers shortly after you were first hired. You might feel ashamed of this event and think people have used it as a means of defining their image of you. You might think they were silently judging you for it. Your idea that they were doing these things is not conclusive proof that this actually happened. This is your assigning feelings and actions to people when these things might not actually be true.

Think about how you feel when you see a person falling down. Do you look at them with coldness and judgment, or was your first thought to check and see if they were okay because you were worried about them? The answer was probably the latter. You probably felt sympathy embarrassment for them because your mind went back to a time when something similar happened to you. That is because you are an empathetic person. Most people are this way. If someone is willing to hold the fact that you fell down and possibly hurt yourself against you, how much should you value the opinion of someone like that?

Don't be concerned with the opinions of someone who is known to be or has shown you to be the type of person who has no care for or even carries distaste for others. This is not a person who will enrich your life in any way. They might act like they have such a superiority over others, but in reality, they don't. A person scoffing at other people doesn't make them better than everyone else. In fact, this is the exact type of person you want to stay away from. They will be toxic to your life. You will have to be isolated from the world in order to keep them in your life because they will not want to have any connections with the outside world. They will want you to cut your ties with it too. A good person does not ask you to keep yourself locked away from everyone else.

If someone says something rude to you, it will naturally hurt your feelings. It damages the natural human want to be a person who is liked by people and thought of as a good person. In times like these, it is very important to remember the good things people have said to you. Do not place importance on this person that does not exist. Also, remember that they might be having a bad day and are taking it out on you. This is not to excuse their behavior, but to help you to not personalize it. Also, think about what kind of person this is. Are they the type of person who frequently speaks ill of other people? If this is so, you are just the current recipient of their chronic anger. What they say about you should be taken with a grain of salt. You probably don't listen to the rude things they say about other people and are incensed by it, so stand up for yourself in the same way. Your opinion of your friends would be changed based on the words of someone else. Don't let your self-worth be diminished by someone else.

There might be people you need to cut out of your life. This is a hard realization to come to, especially if you have known them for a long time and are emotionally invested in them, but if they are doing your life no good, you need to set them free. You can wish them well, but you need to do it from afar.

Here are a few signs; it is time to let go.

- They criticize you all the time. You don't feel like you can make the right move around them, and you find yourself feeling self-conscious.

- They bring an excessive amount of drama into your life. They consistently are fighting with you or someone else, and it makes it so that you hardly have a peaceful moment.

- They are a control freak, and they try to tell you what to do with your life. They feel entitled to make decisions about what you are going to do with your life. You feel like you have to run everything you do by them for their approval.

- It is a one-sided friendship. You are there for them when they need it, but when you are in need of support, they are nowhere to be found. This shows they are a selfish person. This behavior will never change. Even if you get angry at them for it and they apologize, it will always end up the same.

- They are too needy. We all run into problems, but if someone is always in a desperate situation and needs you to pull them out of it, they are not a friend. They are a leech.

Before you go to bed, ask yourself, "Have I done everything I can do to improve myself and my life?" If the answer is no, the answer is not to get out of bed and try to stay up until a disturbing hour coming up with something to do. It is also not to beat yourself up about it. The answer is to acknowledge that you didn't put in the effort you could have today. Then you must forgive yourself and get a good night's sleep, acknowledging the fact that you cannot get anything accomplished by staying up and dwelling on what happened today. Recharge your body so you can do more tomorrow.

When we get into a habit of overthinking, we have a tendency to do a lot of stressing about what has happened in our lives and what is going to happen in the future. This anxiety paralyzes us so that we cannot actually do anything that would be productive. You will need to retrain the way you approach a crisis. Eliminate thoughts that serve no purpose.

This is what is meant by being proactive as opposed to reactive. When a person is behaving in a reactive way, they do not take charge of their life. They let other forces control what happens to them and then get upset when nothing is going the way they want it to. A reactive person plays an active role in their own life. If they are unhappy, they do not sit there and stew, wishing things could be different. They think, "how did I get myself into this situation, and what can I do to get out of it?"

Let's say you are having financial troubles. It's easy to get into a mode where you are panicking about it and angry that you do not have any extra money to spend on yourself and are struggling just to get all of your bills paid on time. However, this approach will ensure that you will never get out of your financial slump. Do not let the feelings of hopelessness and frustration take over. First, you need to assess your financial situation and figure out the first steps you can take to make it better. Are there things you're spending a little too much money on? Are you eating out too many nights a week? Are you subscribed to a magazine you never read anymore? Do you steep prices every month for TV programs you don't watch anymore? If so, there are some easy fixes right off the bat. You can cancel these subscriptions and make the decision not to eat out as much and cook dinner for the night. Already, you have done things which will put more money into your pocket. Budgeting will go a long way in helping you with financial troubles. Figure out exactly what you can spend on a weekly and monthly basis without getting into trouble. Next, make sure you are performing in your job at the best rate you possibly can. You can become discouraged by a lack of money, which makes it tempting to put in the minimum effort at work, but that is counterproductive. Wake up early in the morning. Make sure you look nice. Look at the part of the job you want, not the job you have. It is an old saying, and it has aged well. Go the extra mile on your projects. Ask your boss, "Is there anything else I can do to help?" When they request something of you, don't act like it's killing you. Respond enthusiastically and with a smile on your face. When there needs to be a volunteer to do something, raise your hand. In time your boss will notice how much effort you are putting in and the ways in which you are stepping up, and he or she will have this in mind when it comes bonus time and when they're thinking about who to promote. Also, think of alternative jobs. Many people do freelance projects online to supplement their income. This will give you a little extra money, so you don't feel like you are just barely keeping your head above water. If you do all of these things, before you know it, you will no longer be struggling just to make ends meet.

You are not trapped. You might be bound to certain patterns for a period of time, but you always have a say in what happens in your own life. Do not ever let any other force on earth take your power away.

CHAPTER 5:
SOCIAL MEDIA AND HOW TO KEEP IT FROM CAUSING YOU STRESS

Social media has opened many doors for us. People can now even find work online. It has also been the source of a number of problems in people's communications with one another. While social media helps us get in touch with people, we wouldn't ordinarily be able to reach; it also causes more chances for conflict. In text messages, it is much easier for words to be misunderstood.

Using social media to reach out and connect to others is good. Using it to have conflicts is not. Your anxiety will launch up to the high heavens if you consistently argue with others over social media. Every aspect of your life will be interfered with. You will have a hard time getting to sleep because of the constant buzzing of your phone. You will not properly prioritize your work because your mind will be preoccupied with coming up with your next reply. Your physical and mental health will suffer because you are not getting proper sleep, and your other avenues of self-care will not be given the attention they deserve. When you are having an argument with a friend, constant anxiety is a given. This will only be amplified if you are constantly replying to them. You may think you need to do this because the only way you can get through it is to talk about it, but this is not true. Sometimes continuing the fight will only make everyone involved more upset. You are both tired and have spent too much energy on this. You are also feeling annoyed with one another which makes everyone more prone to saying things they don't mean. Nothing productive will come of this discussion at a certain point. There is something to not going to bed angry, but there is also something to be said about the idea that both parties have had it. In fact, sometimes getting some sleep will change your perspective on things. Letting some time pass before you speak to each other again can make it so that both of you can approach the conflict with a clear head.

Social media arguments have a way of going around in a circle to where all parties involved make the same points, and the conflict never reaches a point where it is resolved. There is definitely a different way people have conflict online as opposed to in person. Even if you are not anonymous, there is still a sense of safety that comes with being behind a keyboard. You do not have to see their facial reactions to what they say. You don't hear their tone of voice. The only thing you feel like you are responding to is words on a screen. In this way, it could be said that we dehumanize the people we are talking to online. It is easy to forget that this is someone we care about, and that makes us resort to something known as right-fighting. This is when people are having a conflict and do not behave in a way that moves toward reaching the productive ending to it. Instead, their main concern is proving they are right, and the other person is wrong.

Not only is it easier to get into arguments with someone, but you are also exposed to disagreements between others on social media websites. You get a front-row seat to your friends fighting amongst themselves. The best thing you can do when this is happening is to stay out of it. Do not leave any comments on this thread, even if it is just to tell them to stop arguing. You will wind up only adding fuel to the fire and getting yourself dragged into the situation.

If they try to talk to you about the person, they have a disagreement with, be neutral about it. Do not give them any information about the person or do any bashing of them, no matter what they tell you because it will get back to this person, which will bring you into the fight. Remember that when people are telling you their side of the story in an argument with someone else, you are getting a biased account of the events. Things the other person did will be exaggerated while the things they did will be minimized or even omitted. This habit is not reserved for people with personality disorders. Everyone does it. We remember our history in a way that paints ourselves in the best possible light, even if it means a little character assassination for others. It's human nature. This means you cannot trust the account of either person. You will not be able to convince them to stop what they are doing. You can only turn their hostilities towards you.

You never know when you are going to get bad news on the internet. That is another reason you should get off of it before going to bed. If you are hit with unpleasant information just before you go to sleep, you will be pulled out of your state of relaxation, and it could be a very long time before you manage to get back into a relaxed state.

You cannot control what other people post on their social media, but you can control what your own account looks like. Your profile will have a direct impact on your mood. In addition, what you post and the comments you write on other people's pages will send a boomerang out. If you post negative things, you will get negativity in return.

When you get other people involved in an argument, you will have their opinions to deal with, as well. Also, think about how volatile an argument is when it is between only two people. Every person you drag into the event takes it up a notch.

If you have a problem with someone, message them directly. Do not do it in a public forum. If you do this, everyone will get a front-row seat to the drama and take part in it. Before you know it, most of the people you know could wind up involved in this argument, which will make it much more than it has to be.

Social media is also something we are prone to use to cause ourselves emotional pain. One of the most common ways we do this is looking at our previous romantic partner's social media profiles after we have been through a breakup. You might be even be tempted to see if they are currently dating anyone and look at their profile. Doing these things will not bring you anything but pain. This is why it is a waste of time. You will be spending precious time looking at your ex's comings and goings and seeing them with their new partner. These pictures and posts will fill you with negative emotions. This will be the time that could be spent working on something that is enriching for you. The more time you spend looking at what they are doing, the less you will be doing, and the longer it will take for you to move on from them.

There is another question you need to ask yourself before you post something- "Is this something I would want a potential employer to see?" That is another problem that comes with social media. You need to worry about who will see what you post. You are not done being interviewed after you are done talking to your potential employers. For many of them, the first place they look while trying to figure out whether or not to hire someone is their profiles on social media websites. If they see pictures of applicants holding or near alcoholic beverages, it will be a turnoff for them. They are also drawn away from profiles where the hateful language is prevalent. If they see that this person is often in the middle of an argument, this applicant's stock will go down.

There are some matters that are better kept private. Social media is not a good outlet for your problems. Even if you don't name the person you are venting about, odds are people will know who you are talking about.

You also run the risk of what you post being misconstrued. That is why you need to think about it when you feel like posting something that has a topic that makes emotions run high. Posting about political or social issues is not advised because it inevitably leads to arguments.

When you put something on the internet, you need to make sure you want this to be something that is permanently accessible. Even when you delete something, there are still traces of its evidence.

When you are posting something that is emotionally charged, wait a minute before you do. Sometimes we say things in moments of anger or another heated emotion, we don't take the time to think about what we are saying and whether or not that is what we really think. It's like the teenager that tells their parents, "I hate you" because they have been grounded. Those were words spoken in anger, and if they really took the time to think about what was in their mind to say, they would realize they do not hate their parents. They are just angry at them because they do not like a decision they made, and they wanted to express that. One moment of satisfaction and vindication later, they feel guilty about what they said because they know it was harsh and hateful. They saw the hurt on their parents' faces and knew they had caused that.

This is something you need to control. When you suffer from overthinking, you are led by your emotions, and you might have a tendency to say things before you have analyzed your thoughts to see if they are accurate. It is important to drop this habit, because while posting covers more ground, what you say to a person is just as permanent. You can't take back what you have said. Even if you say you didn't mean it, the person cannot un-hear it.

When you are using social media, use the same mentality you do for everything else to determine whether what you are thinking of doing is a good idea or not. Ask yourself, "does this do anything good for me? What am I getting out of this? Am I going to accomplish anything out of this, or is this going to be nothing more than a source of drama?"

While social media can be a harmful force, it can also be used as a way to improve your life. Do not forget this. You can find people whose interests are aligned with yours. Explore productive things you could do with the internet. There are many avenues of enriching yourself with it as opposed to having it be a means of stress. Is there some sort of business you've always wanted to run but didn't think you had what it took? You never know what could take off.

Overthinking tries to take so much away from you. It wants you to eliminate anything potentially enriching from your life. Whenever you get an idea, you entertain it for a moment. You think about how great it would be if it would work out, and you see the value in it. Then the overthinking takes over and tells you, "who would want to read/buy that?" and "that's already been done before, it's nothing new." It picks your idea to pieces, and before you know it, you stuff it away and feel embarrassed about ever coming up with it in the first place.

Don't let this happen to your idea. There are flaws in every idea. Think about how many critiques have been done to the most popular movies, businesses, and any other merchandise you can think of, and yet they succeed. Don't listen to the part of yourself that says it is not worth putting out there.

A great way to use social media to nurture your ideas is to join a group that has the same interests as you do. Say you are a writer. There are countless numbers of internet groups for aspiring writers. They show each other samples of what they have written. They ask each other for advice on what to do with a certain idea. Some even have paid opportunities for other people in the group. In fact, that is how many writers find gigs for themselves to buff up their resume.

These groups are also great ways to form social connections. It is always a confidence and mood booster to make a new friend. Just follow the safety rules- don't give away too much information too fast, and most importantly, do not send anyone money. No one needs you to pay them for anything. If they are having financial troubles, they should not be burdening you with it. They should be trying to help their own selves.

Social media is also a great way to work on your career. You can find past professors and employers to connect to and give you references. When you are seeking a job, you want to have as many connections on LinkedIn and other related sites as possible. You want exposure while you are job hunting. Follow groups that are related to your field of interest.

You also need to be prepared to take action if someone on your social media is giving you problems. You do not have to listen to them. Once you block them, you never have to hear from them again. It is recommended that this is a permanent decision. It is an unhealthy habit to have a dynamic with someone where you continually block, unblock, and add them again as a friend. This creates chaos in your life. If you blocked them in the first place, there was a reason for it. They were toxic for you in some way to the point where you felt the need to make it so that there was no way for them to contact you. When you block someone, it means the website itself has enforced that they cannot contact you or even find your profile. This decision shouldn't be made lightly, nor should it be revoked once you have made it. If you do, you will be inviting all of the negativity back into your life that you worked so hard to get out of it.

If someone consistently posts things that are personally distressing to you, but you don't want to completely cut ties with them, there is a way around this. This can also apply for if you like the person, but they fill up your news feed to the point where you can't focus on anything else, and you are sifting through all of their posts to find something you want to read. You can unfollow the person. This way, you don't have to break off the friendship with the person, but you don't have to see everything they post.

If you do unfriend or block someone as a result of them being unkind to you, you do not owe them an explanation. You do not even need to tell them you are going to do it. You do not need to feel guilty about it afterward, either. You did not do it to hurt them. You did it because no one wants to be verbally abused. If someone is sending you hateful or insulting messages, it is verbal abuse as well as harassment, and you have no obligation to tolerate it. It doesn't have to be a certain level of abuse before it counts either. If it makes you feel uncomfortable, it needs to stop.

Also, remember that it does not have to be horrible verbal abuse for it to be justifiable for you to walk away from them. If you are in a group of friends who have a generally negative outlook on life and that brings your spirit down, you not only have a right to leave that group, but it is a responsibility. You do not owe it to anyone to keep a friendship going with someone; it no longer makes you happy. It is a widely accepted belief that if you no longer wish to date someone, you should not be obligated to do so. The same should be applied to friendships. If holding on to a certain friendship is only causing you distressed, and you feel like you are missing out on opportunities to cultivate other, healthier friendships, you need to break off this one. It does not make you a bad person. Sometimes things that were a good fit for your life at one point are now a source of stress. Many things in life have an expiration date. It is not a failure on your part if a friendship doesn't work out. It just means that wasn't supposed to be anymore.

Social media should not be a source of stress. If it is, something needs to change. There is either someone you need to distance yourself from or something you need to spend less time on.

Chapter 6:
Remedies for Overthinking-
Meditation, Mindfulness,
Cognitive Behavioral Therapy

You have a responsibility towards yourself to relieve your anxiety. If you do not get anxiety and overthinking under control, there will be consequences that both your mental and physical health will suffer. The idea that overthinking could have an impact on physical health might be an odd one, but the state of your mental health has a direct impact on your body.

Stress takes a huge toll on your body. When you are anxious and panicky, your heart is pounding, and your throat is clenched. You're trembling and sweaty. This state is hard to sustain, and it becomes exhausting for the body to do so. Being stressed consumes a great deal of energy.

There are a number of physical health problems that can come as a result of prolonged stress. Your immune system is compromised. People who suffer from migraines can trigger this issue more than it needs to be. If you are feeling the effects of stress for too long, you run the risk of having blood pressure problems. You have a greater chance of developing cardiovascular issues. This is because your heart cannot sustain itself, beating at too rapid of a rate in perpetuity. If you have asthma, stress can worsen your symptoms. In fact, it can even bring on an attack. This is also true if you have any form of diabetes. Your symptoms can be enhanced for two main reasons. First, stress is a gateway to unhealthy behaviors such as developing unhealthy eating patterns. It also causes a chemical reaction in the body of someone with diabetes that can cause health issues. It can increase your levels of glucose, which will worsen your symptoms.

You will also suffer from gastrointestinal issues if you are under too much stress for too long. You can experience symptoms that mimic irritable bowel syndrome. If you suffer from frequent anxiety, you might find that you have frequent stomach pain and heartburn. This is because your stomach is unsettled right then. Did you know that when you go into the "fight or flight" mode, certain functions in your body can shut down? This is because when your mind goes into this mode, your body temporarily shuts down certain functions of your body. This is because when you are facing potential danger, the last thing you will be doing is worrying about food. Digestion is unnecessary when your life is on the line. When you go into panic mode, your body thinks you are facing danger.

Stress and anxiety contribute to skin problems and acne. This is why it is so important for teenagers to find ways to keep themselves calm because they are going through a time where they are prone to acne due to hormonal changes and have more moisture in their skin. That is another reason a skin regimen is important. If you are having problems with your skin, it is depressing. You will feel self-conscious which contributes to anxiety. Having a regimen to control skin issues will give you a feeling of control over your life, which is lacking when you suffer from anxiety.

In addition to physical problems, stress exacerbates emotional disorders as well. For people who suffer from anxiety or depression, it worsens and lengthens episodes. Unfortunately, individuals with these disorders are also more prone to becoming stressed, and it affects them more.

Many times the things you want to do because they give you a moment of relief from the anxiety actually help keep the cycle going. An example of this is staying in bed all day because it feels like too much work to get out of bed and start your day. You might think you are more relaxed here than you would be out there in the world. This is an incorrect assumption. Think about how you feel when you hide from the world. Are you calm and relaxed, or are you still feeling anxious at the thought of having to go outside? Avoiding your problems doesn't fix anything, and it doesn't really give you any relief. In fact, it amps up your stress.

You need to get out of the house. When you have anxiety, you will want to stay in bed all day because it seems to give you some relief. How much relief are you getting, though? The anxiety is still there, and you are becoming more and more limited with what you can do in your life.

When you have anxiety, you will have a strong urge to seek reassurance. You might have an insecurity about the shape of your nose and often ask people if it looks bad. You might have a fear of getting into a car accident and constantly question your driving skills. One of the most common reassurance-seeking behaviors is asking one's partner if they truly love them. The problem with seeking reassurance is that it never works in the long run. Take the example of someone who doubts their partner's love for them. They bombard them with questions and tests to prove their feelings are what they say they are. When they "pass," it might give the other person relief for a little while, but then the doubt will always come back. Later they might think, "What if they just said that and don't mean it?" or "What if they meant it yesterday, but not today?"

Don't be fooled. Reassurance will never be permanent, and you will start to frustrate the people around you because they feel like they are having the same conversation over and over again, and they're right. They will even begin to feel harassed.

Cognitive behavioral therapy, or CBT, can help you to combat overthinking. The goal of CBT is to retrain your brain and repair negative and unhelpful thinking patterns. It isn't to change you as a person. You don't need to alter your personality traits. You just need to change ways you see the world that might no longer serve a purpose. It might have aided you in surviving a situation that was unnatural, but now in the world outside of that situation, it is harming you. For example, if a person grew up being taught that technology was wrong would have a hard time navigating through the modern world. We use technology for almost everything. It is how we find places and people. In almost any career path you pursue, there will need to be at least a fundamental understanding of it and how to use it. It is not wrong if it is used for good things, just like anything else in this world. They would need to be told that while there are pitfalls to watch out for with technology and how to avoid them, it can also be a very beneficial aspect of their lives.

It is not a sign of weakness or admission of defeat to get into therapy. In fact, it is a way of fighting for your life because you want a better future for yourself. It is said that change comes from within. If you want your life to change, you have to make it happen.

These thinking patterns do not develop in a vacuum. There is a source to them, usually either from personal experience or from someone teaching you to think this way. As an example, if you were stung by a bee while at a swimming pool when you were young, you might develop a fear of being near a pool. This is because your brain can sometimes be faulty. It can make associations between events that are not actually there. Your brain used the fact that you were by a pool when the bee stung to base its assumption that you were stung because of the location you were at. In reality, you can be attacked by a bee anywhere, and you had nothing to do with it. You might even understand this intellectually, but when you get near a swimming pool, you feel anxiety about a potential bee sting.

These sorts of distorted thinking patterns can apply to more serious matters that affect every aspect of your life. Many times, people who overthink do this because they grew up in a household where they could not rely on the mood to ever stay the same for any long period of time. Their house was chaotic in one way or another. Perhaps they had a parent who was a serial dater, and so they saw people come in and out of the house. They might have had a parent who was prone to rages, and they never knew what would set them off next. One way or another, it was impossible for them to predict what would happen next in their life. That is why they try to go to the worst-case scenario before it happens.

In the case of a person who had a parent who had a short temper, cognitive behavioral therapy would help them come to the realization that their parent's rage was not related to any failures of theirs. A child tries to figure out how everything is their fault. If their parent was always angry at them, they might make an assumption about themselves that they are frustrating. They also make an assumption about other people that they are just as easy to anger as their parents.

When a person goes through any form of trauma, there are certain behaviors others might exhibit that remind the person of the traumatic event, and so they will believe history is going to repeat itself. If the person with the rage-prone parent knew an episode was coming because that parent would give them the silent treatment. Because of this, they assume they have said something to anger a person if they do not reply to their message. In this way, they take blame onto themselves that they do not deserve.

This is why you could benefit from therapy. It is not where "crazy people" go. It is where people go when they have had things happen to them that make no sense, and they are trying to make sense of it. It is a productive thing to do.

You need to work on self-help outside of therapy too. Keeping a journal can be effective in reducing anxiety and helping you to stop overthinking. Sometimes our minds are cluttered because we have feelings we haven't expressed, and sometimes there really is no appropriate place to express them verbally. Maybe you don't want to share this thought with anyone or are in a situation where you don't trust anyone you are currently around with your thoughts. When you write something down, you will automatically feel some relief because you got to express yourself. When you see your thoughts written down, it can be easier to sort them out. You also tell a more unadulterated truth when you write. We censor ourselves when we speak. We can become more concerned with communicating in a polite and socially acceptable way than in an honest way.

Meditation is effective in calming your nerves, which will help you to stop overthinking. When you hear about meditation, you probably get a mental image of someone sitting cross-legged and repeating a mantra that has something to do with walking in the light of love. While this is a perfectly valid way to do it, it is not the only one. The great thing about meditation is that it is open to interpretation. As long as you are entering a peaceful state of mind and you let thoughts of your daily life and the outside world go away, you are practicing meditation correctly. You have to find what your version of it is. You might want to sit up, but some people prefer lying down. It can be in a lit area or at nighttime. You can choose a mantra for yourself or be silent. Some people prefer to have silence in the room when they meditate, while others prefer to put on instrumental music.

Another thing you need to think about when you are meditating is not to try to force yourself to get into a relaxed state. This simply does not work. Trying to force yourself to relax will only make you more upset. This is because you are building up a responsibility for yourself to relax, and if you do not manage to do so, you have failed. Thinking of it this way, it is easy to see how you can become more anxious if you try to force yourself to calm down. A big part of meditation and mindfulness is learning to be alright with wherever you are on the path to reaching your goals at the time. If you are still feeling tense after ten minutes of meditating, that is okay. If you fall into a deep trance after a couple of minutes, that is great, but it doesn't mean there is no other option. Everyone is at their own place on their own personal ladder. Some days you will do better than others. There will be days you are not on top of your game, and your best bet will just be to give yourself a break and try again tomorrow. It is counterproductive to give yourself a hard time for what you have not done, and it is the opposite of mindfulness.

What qualifies it as meditation is the fact that you are focusing on the present and inwardly towards yourself. You are not thinking about when a project is due or about what conflicts you might be having with someone. You are not thinking about anything you did in the past or need to do in the future. You're not worrying about someone else's problems. You're not trying to do anything for anyone but yourself.

You don't always have time to do a guided meditation or yoga, so what do you do if you only have a few minutes?

First, focus on your breathing. If you are struggling with an anxiety attack, you are likely not monitoring your breathing. If it is too rapid and shallow, this will contribute to your anxiety. Breathe slow and deep. While it will not take your anxiety or what is causing it away, it is a start. It will also require some of your focus to be off of whatever is upsetting you.

That leads to another point. Try to focus on something else. While it may feel like your anxiety won't let you think about anything else, this is not true. Because you have been living with it and suffering from it for a long time, it is easy to think anxiety is an all-powerful force. In fact, it only has the power you let it have. For example, if you feel the urge to cancel a plan you've made with your friend out of the fear that you'll be overcome with anxiety, you've given away your power. The same goes for if you break up with someone because the relationship is progressing, and that is frightening for you. You are teaching it that it can make you do anything and take anything away from you. Go back to the plan you made with a friend. Imagine you have anxiety, but you decide you're going to follow through with your commitment and walk out the door anyway. This is showing the anxiety you are the one in control. As you spend time with your friend, your mind is also distracted from yourself for a little while. The things you were worried would happen don't end up happening, and then that shows you that your anxiety isn't a predictor of the future.

While you are overcoming your overthinking problem, you need to focus on your own recovery and no one else's. It is not selfish to put other people's problems on the back burner and prioritize your own needs. It is the right thing to do as well as the responsible thing. No one knows exactly what you need except for you. The word "selfish" has been villainized, and while there is such thing as narcissism and you don't want to get to that point, you also want to be selfish. Let's redefine what that word means. It does not mean you are willing to walk all over people to get what you want, no matter what it costs them. It doesn't mean you see other people as pawns to use to get what you want. Selfish means you think about what the personal cost would be to you before you do something. It means you make decisions that are good for you. It means you are not willing to settle for less than what you want and that you hold people to standards. It means you expect good treatment from other people. It does not even need to mean you hold ill will towards others or that you would use them in a nefarious way.

While you want to focus on where you want to be, think about where you are currently, and what the immediate next step you need to take is. It can be daunting to think about your ultimate goal, and it can actually deter you from taking steps to reach it. Overthinkers are vulnerable to falling into a thinking trap where they imagine a scenario for their life that they would prefer to have, but see it as too much work. They don't see it as possible for them to reach, and they write it off as a fantasy.

As an overthinker, you might discourage yourself from trying to get what you want because you feel like that would work for other people, but it wouldn't for you. You might feel like there is a conspiracy that the world has against you to keep you from getting to the places you want to go to. This is a false belief, and it is negative self-talk. It is also a form of overthinking because you are creating scenarios that do not exist. It is easy to get discouraged when you've had a few disappointments. It might feel like these events were directed at you, but they were not. You might see someone else in a good place, but you don't know how hard they had to work to get there, and the conditions they were living in before they got there.

It's like when you compare the city you live in a city you visit for a few days. Of course, the one you're visiting is going to look better because you were only there for a short time, and you were exposed to the best features of it. You don't have the history with it that you do with your hometown. You might think the people in this city are kinder, but you are only meeting them on a superficial level. They are strangers that you will never see again, and you are comparing them to people you have known for years or maybe even your whole life. You don't have responsibilities like a job and housework in this city. You have the whole day to go site-seeing, and you're probably staying in a hotel where someone else will be doing all of the cleaning for you. Thinking about it this way, it might seem unfair now to compare the two cities.

The opposite of overthinking is being content. This means you accept your life and yourself for what both things are, and that you do not spend your life anticipating tragedies. Have you ever heard the term "no news is good news"? This means unless you are told otherwise, assume things are alright.

CHAPTER 7:

RETURNING TO SELF-CARE

It is important to take care of yourself while you are trying to recover from overthinking and anxiety. This means you have got to relax. For people with anxiety, it can feel almost impossible because it has probably been a long time since they have felt relaxed. In fact, it can be unsettling to feel relaxed for them because it is unfamiliar. The longer you ignore your need for self-care goes on, the direr it will get. If you don't have the time to relax, you can at least tide yourself over until you can focus on yourself. If you are feeling tired at work, close your eyes for just a few minutes.

Check how you are doing physically because your physical and mental health goes hand in hand. It's easy to not be feeling well for a long time and not realize it or push it to the back of your priority list because you are trying to push through and get through the days.

Take advantage of supplements made of natural oils and minerals that are designed to help bolster your immune system, improve your cognitive function, increase your energy levels, fight infections, and overall improve your health. The vitamin B12 gives you energy, allows you to be more productive, and help you if you are just plain not feeling your best. What makes it better than other remedies for low energy levels is that it isn't a forceful boost to your energy. It doesn't make you hyper for a period of time only to give you a crash later, nor does it make it difficult for you to go to sleep. You simply feel like you are more woken up. You feel like you are just waking up after a good night's sleep. If you are having trouble sleeping, melatonin is a natural remedy. Just as B12 doesn't force you awake, melatonin doesn't make you crash hard. You are lulled to sleep, and when you wake up the next morning, you are feeling refreshed, whereas, with other sleeping medications, you might wake up in the morning feeling tired because the effects have not let you go yet.

As an overthinker, you probably spend much of your day grappling with a multitude of worries. Arrange a certain time in the evening where you put away your worries until tomorrow. Save them for a time when you can actually have an impact on them. Also, figure out the ones that are necessary and the ones that do nothing for you but cause you stress.

Make a personal rule to not let something cause you stress unless it is actually happening. You've probably heard the phrase, "we'll cross that bridge when we get there." That means we'll deal with that problem when it arrives and no sooner, and if it never happens, we will never worry about it.

Overthinkers are masters at borrowing trouble. They can create problems for themselves that do not have to exist. For example, if your car is having trouble, you can give yourself a panic attack thinking of how expensive it could wind up being and worrying about if the car is even fixable. Find out how much the repairs cost first. Go on the assumption that whatever is wrong with the car will be fixable. Think about it this way. If it does turn out to be something serious, by the time you get to the point where you find out this information, you will have worried yourself into a frazzle. This means you will have rendered yourself completely ineffective and unable to figure out how to get yourself out of the situation you have worried so much about. No amount of stressing out can prevent a situation. It only takes energy away from you. If you do not give yourself a panic attack about it, then you will be able to take on the situation while you are still fresh.

You need to redirect your thoughts about the situation. Instead of going to "this is the worst thing that could ever happen" or "this is going to ruin my life," focus on this thought instead:

"What is the first step I need to take to get myself out of this situation?" Don't even trouble yourself with the overall solution at first. Just think about how you are going to get through today. Think about paying off the immediate amount.

Let's think about what it means to practice self-care. It could be argued that the root of self-care is getting proper sleep. Every other aspect of your life will take a hit if you are not sleeping well. The timing of your sleep is just as important as the number of hours you get. Let's say you don't fall asleep until 4 in the morning. You probably won't wake up until around noon, so you've already lost half of your day. You will still be groggy, and it'll probably take you longer yet to get out of bed, and even then, you will feel a very low level of energy. It will be all you can do just to get the bare minimum done.

You need to put away your phone before you go to bed. If you don't, there will be a few problems. For one, you will be tempted to play around on your phone and check your social media newsfeeds, and it is easy to lose track of time when you do this. You might look up, and it's 1 in the morning. Then you will need time to fall asleep because no one does the minute they close their eyes.

Do not bring up heavy or upsetting discussion topics late in the evening. If it hasn't come up by then, and no one's life is in danger, it can wait until the morning. Big discussions tend to take an hour to resolve, two if it's a particularly hefty one. If you started it at eight in the evening, you might not be done with it until nine or ten. Then you will have a hard time getting to sleep because when your mind is restless, your sleep will be fitful.

Self-care also means doing things that make you happy. Pick up a hobby. Remember, trying something out doesn't mean you have to stick with it forever. You can take one painting class, decide you don't like it, and never go to another one. Nothing will be lost from trying something.

You often hear "I need a mental health day" as a joke, but there is something to it. Sometimes in our daily lives, with all of our responsibilities, we can become burned out. Just like a cell phone needs its battery recharged, we need our mental battery recharged.

There is no right or wrong way to take a mental health day. It is all about what you want to do. During this type of day, you do not have any responsibilities, and you don't need to think about them. Only do things that make you feel good. It is advisable to avoid too much time on social media during a mental health day.

Establishing good habits for yourself is key to overcoming anxiety and overthinking. If you don't take care of yourself, your defenses are compromised. You are more prone to having physical illnesses, and you will not feel as good about yourself. This means taking pride in your appearance.

Putting effort into your appearance doesn't mean you have to dress in ways that are not you. If you are a woman who doesn't like to wear makeup, you don't have to start doing it. You can look perfectly fine without wearing anything you don't feel comfortable with. In fact, it is cautioned against to try to do that. Then you will feel self-conscious and like everyone is staring at you, which will be the catalyst for an overthinking episode.

What it means to take care of your appearance is to put time and effort into it. When we get into ruts of depression and anxiety, we have a tendency to press the snooze button as many times as possible. Then, when there is no more time to lie in bed, we'll get ready as quickly as we can, and it will be a blur. This means there's no thought put into what you are going to wear, and there's no time to fix your hair other than to run through it a couple of times with a brush. You might not even have time to take a look at yourself in the mirror before you go. This is demoralizing because you know you are not looking your best and are worried others will notice. It will inhibit your confidence when talking to others and might even prevent you from talking to others.

Some people like to pick out what they are going to wear the next morning. This can help you feel more prepared for the next day and gives you one last thing to think about in the morning. Then you have more time to dedicate to other aspects of your appearance. Create some sort of skin ritual. You will start to see results quickly. Learn about different things you can do with your hair and find out what hairstyles work the best with your face shape and which ones you find appealing.

Taking care of yourself also means taking care of the space around you. It is said that a cluttered room is a sign of a mind that has chaos going on inside of it. That is why de-cluttering your environment is so important. When your house is messy, you will feel uncomfortable inside of it. It can get to a point where you have to go through a lot of trouble to navigate in your own house because of the clutter. You have to walk around and step over things. It will increase your stress to have to go through an obstacle course just to walk around in your own home. It is depressing to look at a messy house because you are living in a space you are not pleased with. Instead of your house being a place to come to at the end of the day and find relief from as you leave your worries behind for the day, you come to see a place that has a chaotic energy and that you are ashamed of. You will avoid having any company over and you will dread when you have to let someone in your house, like a repairman, because you are worried about what they will think when they see the state of your house (this is not good for those who overthink, whose shame about the state of the house will last long beyond when the repairman leaves).

There is an impact the energy in the room can have on you. This does not have to carry a spiritual meaning. Have you ever almost gone to a restaurant, but you looked at the people you were with, and you all decided to leave and find somewhere else to go eat because there was something that felt weird about the place? That is what it means to have positive or negative energy. Sometimes it is called the "vibe" or "juju" a person or place gives off. When you have clutter in your house and have not managed its upkeep in a while, the place you live in will have negative energy. It will not be conducive to living a healthy lifestyle and being productive. The way you keep your house sets a tone for the way you live your life. If you regularly clean the space you live in, you will feel more confident about yourself. You will start to enjoy being at home.

There is something to the phrase "fake it until you make it." Even if you are faking it, you are choosing to dwell on something that is beneficial to you rather than something that is harmful. Have you ever been having a bad day, but one of your friends invited you to go out with them, and you decided to take them up on the offer? At first, it might have felt contrived to go out and pretend to be having fun. There was a part of you that wanted to keep wallowing in your sorrows. However, since you were hanging out with your friend and talking to them about things that were unrelated to whatever was bothering you, you didn't have time to devote all of your time to that. After a while, there came a point where you decided you'd rather have fun with your friend than think about what was upsetting you, most likely something you had little to no control over.

If you turn away potentially good things to marinate in the bad things, they will be the only things that come your way. That is why sometimes you will have to do things for self-care and improvement even if you don't particularly feel like it at that time. At first, you will resent doing it because you have to muster up all of your strength and willpower to do things you don't want to do. I can assure you, though; your feelings will change when you start to see the results of your efforts. For example, doing housework is no fun for anyone, especially when it has been a little while since you've done it. It might feel like you will never get it all done. That is why you start with a small but firm commitment- I'm going to go through the clutter in my bedroom and get rid of anything I don't need anymore. When you get it done, you will already see a difference in the room. You are no longer burdened by having things in your space that serve no purpose other than being something you have to sift through to find the things you do want.

It is easier said than done to return to good habits. You might think, "Of course, I don't choose things that are bad for me." When we let go of our power over our own lives, we get into a mentality where we think bad things just happen to us that are beyond our control. We continue to have the same types of relationships, and in other aspects of our lives, there are things left to be desired.

If your friendships and relationships often end badly, take a look at the patterns in how they ended and the faults in these people's characters. Maybe they all had a temper. Maybe they didn't have much going for them and didn't put a lot of effort into their lives. Sometimes we don't realize that we are gravitating towards a particular type of person because even if it is not a healthy relationship, it feels familiar and so we know what to do. The moment you realize you are seeking out the wrong kind of relationships, that is when you can start to change your life.

Sometimes people are tempted to use alcohol to solve their problems. As a disclaimer, drinking socially is not a problem. Having a glass or two of wine in the evening can take the edge off and even be beneficial to your blood pressure. It becomes a problem when you are dependent on alcohol. This means not dealing with your problems other than to have a drink to not think about them. If you consistently feel hungover, it is time to cut back. You do not need to feel ashamed of yourself if you have gotten into a rut where you are drinking a little too much. Everyone who has been alive on this earth has had times like these. You just need to remind yourself that alcohol is not meant to be a solution to a problem. In fact, it is supposed to be something that makes you have fun.

Self-care also means finding yourself. This means finding out what you want to do with your life as well as your own personal identity and owning it. People who suffer from overthinking have difficulty getting in touch with their authentic selves because they are overly concerned about what others think of them. This is known as people-pleasing. It might sound like the trait of a kind person on the surface, but in reality, it is something you want to stay far away from. It will get you taken advantage of, and it is actually an insincere way to go about life. Even "benevolent" deception is still deception.

Think about it this way. You have a friend who really enjoys eating at a certain restaurant. They often request that the two of you go there, but you don't care for the type of food they serve. Going there feels like a chore to you, and you dread going out to eat with them because you know they are going to suggest this restaurant. You keep this inside because you feel like you are being nice by going with them to a place you don't like, but is it really that nice? You are harboring resentment towards them for always taking you somewhere you don't want to go, but you have not given them any sign that you are feeling this way. They might think you like it as much as they do and look forward to the times where you go to this restaurant. They might even think you regard it as a special place for the two of you.

It would be very easy to tell them they could go to it on their own time, but you don't want to go there. You have a responsibility to do this. It will not be easy, especially if this dynamic has been going on for a long time, but you have to do it. The longer it goes on, the more resentment you will have built up for your friend. No one can read your mind. You may think you are preserving the friendship by not telling them you don't like their favorite restaurant, but you actually need to tell them the truth to save your friendship. This may not seem like it is a part of self-care, but it is. Managing your friendships will strengthen your mental health dramatically.

Chapter 8:
Managing Anxiety Flare-Ups

The unfortunate truth is that once you decide you're going to stop overthinking and take the steps to break the habit, this is just the beginning. Changing something you've always done isn't a clean break. It isn't like uninstalling a game on your phone, where it is gone, and there is no trace of its existence. You've been repeating these patterns in your mind for many years now, maybe even for as long as you can remember. Sadly, you will experience anxiety flare-ups while you are learning to stop overthinking.

You need to be prepared for some strange sensations when you take steps to stop overthinking and overcome anxiety. You will feel somewhat afraid the first time you are not experiencing anxiety. It will be discouraging because you have done all this work to stop feeling so uneasy all the time, and then here it is happening all over again. Here is why this is happening to you.

You do not need to be afraid of flareups. It does not mean you are going to slip back into where you were before. It just means your symptoms need some attention. Think about how sometimes you get a cold. Your nose is stuffy, and your temperature is a little warmer than it should be. It doesn't mean you are seriously ill. It just means you need some cold and flu medication.

People have an innate fear of the unknown. When you're in a place that is unfamiliar to you, you feel a sense of vulnerability. You might even feel some urges to return to your state of anxiety because while it's unpleasant, it's at least familiar. If your mind isn't cluttered with fear, what comes next?

I'll tell you what comes next. You will feel content more often. Those tender moments with your friends and family will not be sabotaged by doubts and insecurities. You will feel free to explore what you could be in the future. You'll explore new friendships and relationships without a burden on the back of your mind calling everything they do into question.

Always keep in mind that every bout of anxiety has an expiration date on it. It will pass. Your body will not allow you to go on in a perpetual state of distress. Even if the feeling comes back after a while, this particular episode will have no choice but to come to an end. At some point, your adrenaline will run out. Essentially, you will become too tired to be anxious.

Remember what is really going on around you. Do not listen to the distressing thoughts. Look around you. This is what is really happening. You are not in any danger, no matter what the anxiety is trying to tell you. No catastrophic event is right around the corner.

You can take steps to break yourself out of a bout of anxiety. Recognize when you are overthinking. Say you are coming home from a party, and your mind is starting to wander off to offhand comment you made throughout the event. You begin to pick them apart, deem them embarrassing, wonder what people must think of you now that you said it. You start wondering if they are still thinking about these things.

This is where you need to stop and break out of this vicious cycle. You might even need to say the word "stop" out loud to stop the thoughts in their tracks. Resist these thoughts. Do not sink into them. You might have heard the story about deciding which wolf you feed because that one will become the stronger one. Do not feed the part of your mind that creates doomsday prophecies and hurls insults at you.

You do not owe distressing thoughts' attention. Imagine someone was sending you messages with the same ugly remarks your mind is telling you. It probably wouldn't take long for you to block them, and you would write them off as a hateful and vicious person. So why should you let thoughts in your head torment you with impunity?

It is no easy task to change the way the voice in your head speaks to you, but you can start by deciding you are not going to listen to negative self-talk. This is a term to describe when you are saying things to yourself that are put-downs. When you listen to this voice and accept the words as true, it is easier for you to get taken advantage of by other people. It can also cause you to interpret other people's actions in a different way from what they intended them to be. For example, you might see someone looking at you because they think you look nice today. Because of the negative self-talk, you might think they are looking at you for the opposite reason, that they think you look bad.

The beginning of ending negative self-talk is simple. When one of those thoughts comes into your mind, say to yourself, "That's not true." Stand up for yourself the same way you would stand up for a friend who was being bullied. Do not bully yourself.

You will never get satisfying answers to the questions in your mind. You will never be able to figure out whether or not they were fond of a comment you made. They might not even remember you said it. People tend to forget most of the content of the conversations they have with other people. If they do remember it, they might think about that moment in a different way from how you see it. They might have found what you did endearing. They might even be feeling self-conscious about the impression they made.

There are a few people who will intensely like you. Some people you meet in your lifetime will dislike you. However, most people will be fairly indifferent. This is not to make you feel like you do not make a difference in other people's lives. This is to show you that you are not being looked at with a microscope. People are not watching you carefully for your next mistake.

To leave overthinking in the past for good, you need to turn your focus to yourself. Worry about your own life. The people whose opinions truly matter are in your life and make time for you. If you never see this person, why should their opinions of you matter?

Get closer to the people in your life who have your best interests at heart. Many times when we are in a great amount of distress, we fall into the habit of putting more effort into relationships that are unhealthy for us and drift away from the ones who could be conducive to our mental well-being. Do not worry if it has been a long time since you two have spoken. Just send them a message. If there was no big falling out and the two of you just drifted apart as a result of life happening, you do not need to make a big deal about how long it has been since you have spoken. Just tell them you want to see how they've been, and you have missed talking to them.

When we exercise good habits, unhealthy ones become weaker. The reverse is also true. This is why you need to make a decision about which one you are going to encourage. If you want to live in a constant cycle of feeling guilty as a result of one moment of gratification, you give in to the bad habits. No one wants to feel like this, but if you put time into bad relationships and habits, this is what will happen.

It takes willpower to practice good habits and stay away from the bad ones. You will need to become a master at impulse control. Overthinking can become addicting at a certain point. No one does something because there are no upsides to it. Even if it is an unhealthy one, there is some benefit to what we do, no matter what it is. In the case of overthinking, we feel a false sense of control. We analyze everything to the highest degree because it gives a feeling of security.

Breaking the habit of overthinking is taking your life back. It takes so much away from you. It takes away moments that could be peaceful. It makes it difficult to sleep and eat. You have probably sabotaged friendships and prospects of romance because a voice in your mind told you to doubt it.

There is a difference between intuition telling you something is off about a person or place, and overthinking trying to limit you. You can become better at distinguishing the two by saying "yes" more often. If the commitment does not take too much out of you and you don't have to risk things in order to do it, say yes. Overthinking causes us to say "no," too often. We're afraid we will fail or make a fool of ourselves, or that we will get our hearts broken and have regrets.

Do not fear regrets. They will happen, but they are not the worst things in the world. One way to overcome the fear of the unknown is to travel. Do not fret if you do not have the money to go on an expensive vacation in an exotic land. It counts as travel if you go somewhere you haven't been to before, or don't go too much. This can mean going to a restaurant you have wanted to try out for a while, but haven't gotten to. If you like it, you have somewhere new to eat at, and if you don't, you can mark it off as a learning experience.

You can start to break out of your shell by doing something spontaneous but risk-free. Go to karaoke night with your friends. Pick a song and get up onto the stage. Don't worry about how you will sound or if you know all the words. Decide on a song people will know and dance to. Have fun while you're up there, and don't be afraid to make a mistake. Overthinking makes us think mistakes are horrible. This is not true. In fact, sometimes the best things in life are mistakes. You might sing the wrong words, and everyone thinks it's hilarious, and it becomes an inside joke between you and your friends. There is also such a thing as a happy accident.

To stop overthinking is to start feeling comfortable with who you are. You don't judge yourself too harshly, and you stop others too harshly as well. You take more control over your life by letting go of the things you can't impact and taking an active role in the things you can't control. It is to stop worrying about what other people are doing or thinking and doing more about your own life. When what others think is in the back of your mind, you live a happier life. When you live a more authentic life, you don't have time to overthink because you are too busy making decisions that benefit you and doing the things you want to do.

It might help you to write down two lists- one including the things that trigger your anxiety and how to know when you are having an attack, and the other being the things that help soothe you. Remember that this is personalized. Things that may not work for other people might be the thing you need to do to wind down after a stressful day. There is nothing wrong with you if soft music doesn't work for you. Maybe there is a particular movie that makes you feel calm, and it is a scary one. There is nothing wrong with that. Overthinkers have a tendency to put themselves in the no-win scenario where they call into question the things they do to reduce their anxiety.

There is a difference between something you do to find some relief from stress and coping. When you use coping methods, you do not address the problem. For example, you have a stressful project to do at work. Coping would be to avoid working on it and instead choosing to surf the internet, which is unhealthy. If you have completed all of your assignments for the day and you watch your favorite show at the end of the day to escape, you are not doing anything wrong. It would even be alright to watch an episode as a way to wind down before you get to work. It becomes coping when you do it to the exclusion of dealing with your problems. The same could be said about eating, drinking alcohol, or using some other form of substance, or playing video games in order to not live your life.

Make sure the things you are doing help you grow and increase your happiness. What we invest time and energy in thrives, while the things we neglect will wither. If you neglect your life, it will wither. If you do not take care of yourself, you will falter. Do not give troubling thoughts more than they deserve. However, you need to know how to fight them.

Dealing with overthinking can be compared to dealing with someone who has a narcissistic personality disorder. In both cases, you have an entity that cannot be reasoned with and is only interested in hurting you. The overthinking part of your brain will not give ground. You can try to tell it something reasonable, like "My friend didn't lie when they told me their car broke down, and they can't hang out today," but it will always counteract your arguments. It will say, "How do you know that? Maybe they were offended by something you said last time you spoke to them, and this is their way of discarding you." Of course, you will want to have an emotional reaction to this, but that will only make the vicious cycle go on and on. Just as a narcissist will gaslight you and try to get you to question your own memory and even your sanity, so will your overthinking.

Gray rocking has become a popular way of dealing with a narcissist. The name speaks for itself. This tactic involves acting as dull and emotionless as a gray rock. You do not engage when they try to get you engaged in an emotionally charged conversation. You need to gray rock your overthinking. Do not give it anything to go on. If it starts telling you, "They didn't respond to your text because they hate you," just say, "Maybe that's so, maybe not. I don't know." Just as the narcissist goes for the victims they can get a rise out of, your overthinking wants to drag you into a cycle where you try to reassure yourself, and it rips your argument to shreds so you are fumbling around desperately trying to come up with another one so it can do the exact same thing to it. Your distress serves as the narcissistic supply for the anxiety, so if you do not give it that supply, it will not be as interested in you. You will not be an easy target.

Anxiety and overthinking will be the dominant force as long as you play by its rules and live in fear of its ever-looming threats. However, anxiety has no power outside of your own head. It cannot make bad things happen to you. You are the one with the power, and this is the start of the rest of your life. A year from now, overthinking could be a distant memory.

CONCLUSION

Overthinking is not impossible to overcome, but it isn't easy. You will need to employ every resource you have. It is recommended to take up meditation and how you do that is open to interpretation. You should also consider cognitive behavioral therapy because its goal is to retrain your thoughts to become healthier and more productive. You will need help from others to overcome this because if you've been doing it for most of your life, it's become automatic by now. Overthinking isn't something you can just quit overnight.

Just because you've had the habit of overthinking until now, doesn't mean you can't stop now. Habits can be broken, even if they have been practiced for a long time. It will take more than just contradicting these thoughts once to get rid of them. You will need to hold yourself accountable, which means learning how to notice when you're overthinking and tell yourself to stop. You might even have to say it out loud to break the spell.

Part of your recovery will involve accepting that you can't change the past or predict the future. There is no going back and undoing what has already happened, and no one knows what is going to happen in the future. You can prepare for it and hope for the best, and that's the extent of your control over the future. There is one thing you can impact, and it's the present. You can choose to be content right now and leave tomorrow's worries for tomorrow.